Gas Deities

Other poetry by Ed Wright

When Sky Becomes the Space Inside Your Head, 2012
The Empty Room, Vagabond Press, 2002

Gas Deities

Ed Wright

PUNCHER & WATTMANN

First published in 2020
Published by Puncher and Wattmann
PO Box 279
Waratah NSW 2298

http://www.puncherandwattmann.com
puncherandwattmann@bigpond.com

NATIONAL
LIBRARY
OF AUSTRALIA

A catalogue entry for this book is available from the National Library of Australia.

ISBN   9781925780758

Cover design by Miranda Douglas
Typesetting by Morgan Arnett
Printed by Lightning Source International

Contents

Baked Gods 1: Miracle Child

Carol reckoned she had baked a little god,
a miracle something so fine could rise
on the yeast of the old man's beery jism.
He soon racked off to the land where misery
shacks up with freedom; in the pinched rooms
of boarding houses he rode the nauseous surf
between the last schooner and the first.
Thoughts of his son were an inspiration to pour another one
and he elbowed his way guilty into the amber limbo
while the little god searched for dadda on the TV soaps.
The sperm was disowned but mother and son got by,
Carol and her Evan moon, whose dark side never showed
to the maternal light, whose achievements accrued like wrappings
around wounds. The mummified boy grew handsome,
clever, strong, grew to love the shadows,
the smoulder of transgression invisible to (s)mother love.

Carol kept him close,
play dates only from necessity,
and only with the other single mothers,
you can never know a man, the evil behind those smiling fathers,
all sport and surface, their eyes running
from their instincts, the decent ones at least.
Careless once was quite enough.

On weekends he came with her to the real estate
where she collected the rents, scared the tenants,
and thrilled the hungry agents
with her hot but furious loneliness.

Big Phil was the king of sales, a killer
of scales, a taverna lived under his belt.
Another mummy's boy made good,

Phil reckoned Carol's little god might look good
handing out the brochures at the open houses.
Against the instant best friend charisma of
his honey brown eyes, Carol couldn't think
fast enough why no. And so Evan went,
hands on the leather of the Mercedes,
tie and a hasty suit
sitting gawky on his frame.
Son, you've got to look the part.

If Carol could have seen the future,
she would have chained him to his bed.
Her Evan was uni bound, a family first,
he almost won a scholarship to the posh school,
was doing well at the smart school,
was smart enough to be a lawyer,
in dreams that flowered awkwardly
in the bed of Carol's untended intimacy
he was smart enough to join those fatherless men
fighting for primacy in the parliament.
He was first family material,
the hidden streaks risks not cancels,
a hungry by-product of the damaged animal's
will to power over the herd.

Big Phil loved a punt. He sold the dream domestic
then blew it on the pokies or the nags. Saturday arvo
an old one bedder, hardly worth the effort for the big man,
but just around the corner from the TAB,
spring racing just beginning; the season for flutters.
Son, you go on ahead and open up. I'll be there in a minute.
Disaster! The filly breaks a foreleg in the straight
and Phil has dropped the fifteen grand he's promised
for the family holiday. The missus will go ballistic and
his face is red with shame all the way

from the TAB to where Evan is smiling
and a girl is smiling, and her Dad is waiting to make the offer.
Something for her while she studies drama at the uni.
A call to the owner, the deal is done,
Phil has half of his bad bet back: Bali instead of Paris?
He slings Evan 200 to impress him, or his mother.
Later that afternoon the girl rings to say
she'd like to see the flat again
before she heads back to Sydney.
Here's the key, says Phil to Evan.
Do you mind showing her round?
And so he does. And so does she,
in the bedroom, all private school bossy,
she pushes him, backs of his knees against the bed,
then falls on top, mouth to mouth,
the tie comes first, the shirt, his best,
its buttons ripped, she's studying drama,
but will probably become a lawyer,
the belt the pants the boxers
he has no control, she's wearing no undies
has a tattoo of a mouse
with whiskers on her thigh
is amazing wet amazing mischief in her eyes.
Nothing is ever the same again.
Out goes the law. In goes the sell.
Sex-brained on that one reward
and wanting more, a course at TAFE,
suits on the weekend. Carol's
disappointed, but it could be worse –
at least he's not his father
or a member of a cult –
besides everyone's talking property.
There are agents on the bus stops,
on the sides of the busses,
on the TV (if you're still watching),

even in the dunnies at the bowlo.
And now there's a junior agent
destined for greater things:
Evan does it better says the sign.
While Big Phil's at the club,
he's doing the mid-week hard yards
in the new estates with women
who have taken a shine and
arranged for private inspections
while their husbands are in the mines.
Experience is his teacher, and so is porn:
he is the hero of his own Italian movie,
a handsome conduit for the expression of unattended fantasies.
He likes to sit his lovers on the washing machine
and ride the tremble. He loves
the way women wobble, like the way the mind
moves on the verge of big decisions,
like a buyer about to offer,
and because he is the son who can't do wrong,
he doesn't blink when returning husbands,
tense with readjustment, are persuaded
— happy wife, happy life —
to put a deposit on the house.

The carapace grows to an Audi and a studio
in town he rents to foreign students,
(why leave home, says Carol, terrified)
but only girls — the boys are lazy slobs, and besides ...
At work his yellow magnet jumps
up the meeting room whiteboard like a checker
that has read *The Art of War*.
There is envy and Evan enjoys it.
He drives a Disco, skis in Aspen
during summer when the market goes to sleep,
gets his suits and shirts tailormade,

keeps fresh boxers and a crisp white Oxford
hanging in the car in case. Like one Wednesday afternoon
2-bedroom, spa bath, Miele appliances
(his favourite kind of machine)
loggia views over the park, close to all conveniences,
owner in a hurry — transfer to Melbourne —
all reasonable offers accepted, but still the going's slow,
only three parties and no one takes a contract,
then just as he's packing up, a ponytail blond
in active wear, familiar, fit. Don't I know you?
Don't think so, you've probably seen me on the news
— that's it, she reads it —
You look so much better in the flesh
You don't look that bad yourself.
The words are banal but the essence is electric,
the flat's not right but the fuck's fantastic
the sequel even better, then a call:
I have a boyfriend but
we'd like an expert
to talk about houses on the news.

Big Phil is annoyed. He's been on a bus,
in the paper, even radio. But never the TV.
You're not ready. You should have talked to me first.
They'll eat you alive. Young Evan rolls his eyes
and eyes Phil's rolls. Not ready?
Not ready to relinquish top dog, more like it.

Phil's no fool. And he doesn't like losing.
Evan rarely sells a property to a man.
He's seen the women blushing after Evan's opens.
He's heard them asking for him on the phone.
He puts a hidden camera in the bedroom of a house
that Evan's selling, sends an escort for an inspection and ...
Busted! But the big man's luck is out,

real estate's a merry-go-round and the word's round town:
the boy can sell, who cares how he does it?
Sex tapes are just another way to be famous now.
Morality's a happy vendor handing over the commission.
Young blokes should take the chance to sow their oats
before they're yoked and blah, blah, blah.
You don't understand loyalty, Davo,
he tells the principal, who doesn't
so Phil chucks a tanty and tells the young gun's Mum,
who doesn't want to hear it, and slaps his face.
Why would you ever go out of your way
to help someone if that's the gratitude you get,
he shouts, and storms off to join the competition
leaving Evan and his unique selling point
as the firm's new number one.

Screen of Death

When people die they go to television
and audition for their elevation.
Some are extra, others star,
now it doesn't matter.
On the conveyor to the furnace
I dreamed that I might read the news
or sing a song on a talent show
called *What Went Wrong.*
The flames forgot to touch me, but how to sing,
'one minute I was there, the next one gone',
a high note for when the clot exploded
in my brain, sustained like a tragic diva
on the journey up the tunnel
of my last embodied thought:
pancakes hot and syrupy;
the sweet tart slightly ginger pop
of blueberries with cream.
I left my loved ones over breakfast,
now they're on the couch as large as life
and of the earth, waiting, intangible,
channel surfing – for me? –
just outside the screen.

Ghosts are prettier than people,
our blemishes are lessened
by the lost dimension.
On the third week of my death
I rose again from the casting couch
and sang of tinned spaghetti:
May the sauce be with you!
'Sing it like you mean it,' the director snarled,
then they showered me in the stuff.
On the next set they were sequelling

The Sound of Music. Perhaps I
could understudy the Captain
and marry sweet Maria. A nice lady,
who introduced herself as the executive producer,
came over with a towel. 'Have faith,' she said,
'have faith', so I knew as she dabbed
the gunk from my eyes
that we would shoot the ad,
jingle all the way to hell,

again
and again
and again

Bear Hunt

Bears pursue me,
their button eyes
stitched in a factory
are cruel with the boredom
of their making.

Cuddling is futile,
these bears, born vengeful,
will not be deterred,
they are under the doona
they are into my ears
they are inside my sleep,
soft police turned vigilante
egging my creaky sleep criminal,
sweating into the pillows,
as I beat to pulp
(do you ever dream in noir?)
the intruders creeping in
to steal my child.

Night after night after night
I am woken by the
clench of cortisol
and the shame of things
I can't explain:

the hot frustration of my heart;
an impotence from long ago
grown narrative tumours,
revenge fantasies that
defend the wound from cure.

Inside, my pounding,

outside is quiet,
the children are serene.
I am unworthy of their innocence
until this grit subsides.

The bears cast their cold eyes around.
It is crowded where they come from,
the days are long – and who can afford
to waste their rest like this.

I almost detect a smile,
as if my grinding teeth and paranoia
were their coffee and donuts
on the long watch
until they slip back under the covers
where their girl (my girl)
will love them
with her best pretend
again.

Hunger

Starving people are on the television again.
I give money but is that care?
Pay not to be them, pay because
they are a burden on my luck,
cos I'm into lightening up.
30 seconds and they'll be gone
for margarine and beer.
My doctor tells me I gotta lighten up
(well, after the next beer);
it's too easy to say
it's all about the effort,
to tell that starving kid with the
flies on his eyelids
and his belly puffed
into cruel skittle portliness
that character is destiny.

Like you, though, I'm a cognitive miser.
My success was pre-diabetic,
the new me will be lite and easy.

Is charity a kind of vanity?
A shortcut in a sharp suit —
I'm looking good;
or more like aftershave —
I'm smelling good;
is charity lubrication —
I'm fucking good
that girl with the short black
dress and status eyes
who knows how to underplay privilege.
It's all good fun and that matters
because bad fun is just as easy

and everyone has their moments,
like when I see the parents
of the children who are dying
and can't build the difference
and imagine they are mine.

Baked Gods 2: Absence

Mark and I were wondering
if we were going to make it,
might have broken up if not for the house
with both our names on the mortgage,
and the strange cloud of grief around the stillbirth
that bound us with its puzzle, baby Cody,
perfect – he ended before he began.

I didn't want to stay in that death house
any longer than I had to, didn't want
to lie on the nursery floor replaying the unknown,
seeking the moment his little heart stopped,
between the glass of champers at Josie's wedding
and the ultrasound three days later.
Mark had gone back to the gasfields
with a hangover, had a spew in Perth.
Don't worry, I'm sure it's fine he told me,
big softy, whose ear had rested on my belly
listening to the beat, his tears of joy
warm on my skin, but his voice hardening
with the macho armour of the miner's camp,
some dickhead already telling him no doubt
how pregnant women are crazy,
how their hormones get the better of them –
the shit we listen to because
how mediocre they are, these men,
unable to carry life inside them
and thus reduced to culture
(and then reducing culture).
Don't worry, it'll be OK, he said,
catching his hardness and softening, I love you both,
then no answer for ten calls in a row,
sorry I was drilling a hole, if it makes you feel better

why don't you ring the doc and get it checked.

It didn't. Lying there, cold gel on my belly,
the ghost of him on the screen, no sound.
The doctor came in. 'I'm very sorry Mrs Hughes,
but I'm afraid he's gone. Have you got someone
you can call to take you home?'
I willed my mother back from the dead
then called Mark and howled down the phone.
They called me a taxi. Two days later,
Mark held my hand while I delivered Cody: he was beautiful.
They burned him and urned him. We took him home.
I swam against the grief, lap after lap
of the ocean pool. It didn't help.
I walked for miles along the beach. It didn't help.
I stared into the fire at night. There was no wonder.
It will get better the counsellor said, Mark said,
they all said. I'm not a fucking broken chair
that you can fix. It can't be fixed.

Mark wasn't equipped
to travel beyond the practical:
the raw grief terrified him.
He kept it at a distance,
sealed in a box, with the exception
of a hole in the garage wall.
But mine was a monster swell,
a series of freak waves, no boundaries.
He never even got born.

Life is a habit of some force,
but I didn't want to walk out to the
back garden and imagine how
the flowering gums might look in ten years' time –
how he might have looked –

I didn't want to walk out the front
and look at all the other houses
almost the same as mine,
cars in their driveways, the fresh kerbs
of the cul-de-sacs like bones.
I didn't want to wake up to the noise of birds.
As soon as his little heart stopped beating,
my dream went wandering,
life was somewhere else.

~

Odd how we can live in several directions
simultaneously, when without our bodies
we would be nothing but a list of nouns
written in invisible ink. Without his body,
Cody is only a name, an umbilical constellation
of clustered sadness, truncated hopes and unlived dreams.
Odd too while knowing we are only our bodies,
how easily the truth is tossed into the undergrowth.
Sunday mornings waking up alone
(Mark away again) I couldn't bear
the sounds of the kids playing;
the bells of their bikes, their fights,
the bouncing balls on the safe bitumen.
'Go away', I wanted to scream.
Why were they playing, why did they have bodies
when my Cody was in the pantry in his urn?

The days were Netflix without focus,
slabbed and forgotten.
In the darkness that underlaid
the cloud fuzz of the fluoxetine
it came to a point:
kill myself or do something. Anything.

Lacking the bravery
to follow Cody into the unknown
I stumbled out of bed one afternoon
and resolved to sell the fucking house.
Mark was still in WA, keeping the dream alive,
but I wasn't going to ask.

Grief's a sneak – a tap on the shoulder
with an electric prod, the lifelessness in between.
At three o'clock, a knock. Did I flick my hair back as I …
'Evan, please come in.' His eyes were blue.
I'd seen them on a bus coming back from ALDI,
stocked up with cheap rosé and cheese.
'Evan's even better!' it said beneath his head.
Better than who? Better in the flesh.
I could get lost in those eyes, I thought,
if I wasn't already.
Would you like a cup of tea?
Nah just a glass of water, thanks.
Nice place, he said. Why are you selling?
It's time to move on. He didn't press.
Mind if I look around. Guided tour:
kitchen, bathroom, bedroom, study, bedroom.
Cody's empty cot, his name still on it
in cut-out coloured letters. The mist descended.
Is your husband home? His white shirt was
like a giant hanky. Such a wide chest.
His hands were warm.
I'll put together some figures and
drop them round on Thursday afternoon.

Thursday morning I was taking off
one pair of jeans and putting on another
then taking the jeans off and
putting on activewear, casual,

as if I had just been to the gym,
a dash of perfume on the neck, lipstick
for the first time since the funeral.
Odd, which strangers we need to impress.
Some are just cardboard cut-outs in our path,
or faces forgotten by the end of the transaction.
Others are swallowed by their category:
firemen; butchers; obstetricians ...
He had such soft little hands. Guilty!
For a moment I'd forgotten, how could I?
my poor boy, whose only life's inside my mind.
Is he doomed to come and go, like fashion,
like hangovers, like the sun on cloudy days.
The sad shack of my head –
crap place to call his home.

Some people had avoided me,
others overcompensated,
as though this was always
my destiny and would remain so,
as if life can be divided
into the favoured and the enduring.
But Evan's white shirt was stiff
with Preen when he returned
and its freshness trailed me through the house.
I'm sorry about your son. His hand was
on the small of my back as we exited Cody's room.
In the bedroom the sky in his eyes changed,
a glint of mischief, a distraction if not a solution:
that great white hanky of a shirt,
bouncing on the edge of the bed
as if no stain could last forever.

The choice was mine:
more of the impossible same

or a new whatever. I was already
too full of the old consequences to think
beyond the moment, my body, a treacherous dairy,
pulled me towards the future with its desires.
Cody was napping. Mark never entered my mind.

My hand reached up to squeeze his shoulder,
his head bent down for a tippy-toe kiss,
my face fell into his shirt,
whose buttons became undone.
I peeled my active wear and revealed
the woman beneath the seal, my hands
pushed down on his hairless chest.
I gave in to animal grief
and tasted my annihilation
– life is wilder than we think –
I fucked him slowly, crying all the way,
milk pearled on my nipples when I came
and I wondered if I could bear it all again.

Opticals

1

I mistook a ship for an island
stillness is relative
your head is a bag of nuts
weighed down by rocks
life is so confusing
I am not sure
I am in it.

2

Eyes in a moving frame, express
the blur of rapid forest.
Slowing into a station
legs are seen from the lower deck,
their tastes in shoes,
coming home on the upper
the thoughts on waiting faces
you will never see again.

Bears 2

I hear your ringtone in the soundtrack to cartoons
and confuse my frightened forgiveness with revenge.

Where have you been?

At night I dream of violent bears, the children's toys.
There are no pearls from the grit of this sleep,
only the blur of the unreal
tripping up the day.

When someone I must greet walks past
my mind is away, before I know it
I have snubbed them. I cannot call them back.
They have suffered a tragedy, but I cannot call them back.
I have suffered a tragedy, but I can't remember what it is.

Oh childhood! So much second-hand smoke
and photos!

At night the bears are back.

It is madness to run when there are only circles. Still I do.
I am a small screw drilling myself into a piece of wood.
It gets harder every day to get out of bed.

I am a taut cord
whipper-snippering the grass.

The surface of this chaos is so neat,
like hospital corners on a bed.

In sleep the bears surround me, they pummel me
with their ruthless fur, shouting,

"what is the point of being almost human?"

My guilt is indecipherable
from who I am. It is longer than memory,
it is food for bears.

The Collective

A chorus of mosquitos
A shout of mates
A tyranny of idiots
A corruption of leaders
A thing of the rich
A vanity of ambition
A sore of falling short
An immortality of doubt

Gas Deity

Nitrous oxide: about as close
as it gets   to the gods
without sacrifice, the nonsense of origins
a pretty polly epiphany
polyphony cackling through
the wireless speakers of the mind.

It's a shame they don't serve religion at the dentist anymore.
It damages the brain, the wowsers say, and it's true
that religion should be consumed in moderation,
but what's a few cells culled from the mortal billions
while they drill.

My last dentist wore loud shirts
and installed bad crowns in mouths.
His talk of motor yachts as he drilled
and filled was a poor craftsman's
desperate superiority, the man was all enamel,
an anger coated in achievement, my mouth
was his McMansion, his shirt an admission
of life being elsewhere. Probably Hawaii.

My new dentist takes 3D images of my jaw.
There are coloured regions like a rain chart
where the teeth press together:
mountain ranges chowing down
on the unevenness of things,
clenching the inequality of dreams.

Megabytes ride the ether, in the next room
a small mill the size of a budget printer
carves the crown.
We watch it together wearing our smiles.

Who needs gods when you can do this?
He fits it, bakes it, glues it in. So many
almost miracles, so many leaps of reason
to tantalise the understanding.
His assistant gives me the bill.

God is historical and I am on my way to join him.
This dentist is younger than me
and in better touch with the future.
He looks like a movie star and I'm already looking back,
to the old days, when we self-administered religion.
We were stupid then, beginnings seemed endless,
the gods were mostly with us, we found them
when we drove to Maccas and sucked
the nitrous out of ten whipped cream bulbs
in the carpark, then tried to order burgers
from the smiling girls inside
without dissolving into laughter.

Surface Paradise – The Conference Version

My head is full of sex without intent,
it's the bikini overload, the triangles and curves,
If only I were Picasso … the hand that rubs the oil,
but I'm an academic on my lunchbreak at a conference
– some funded happy hours of research points (and powerpoints)
the reverent irrelevance of lipping critical gloss onto
the reduced fat faces of fiction.

It's a mental wrestle to encapsulate an aspect of this
without using a titular colon. The poetics of Ophelia's dimples
darwinismically constructed – sheets of expanding detail
pinned to hunches about vanished realities.
Surface Paradise, we're convening at the Renaissance,
powerless against the pun, a ham omelette with a Danish for brekkie,
though the shit coffee must have come with the American keynote,
and the vegos are shaking their (asparagus) spears.
The gossip spans continents and centuries, no one here
has a clue as to the goings on over there at that time,
but we are making up for lost time with
'The eco-poetics of the British hunt in the work of Thomas Wyatt',
'The thatched roof as desire in the marginalia of Lady Montague'
'The threesome as structural principle in the sonnets of John Donne'.
(A spit roast has been advertised for dinner.)
There is much to admire in the intricacy of these fortresses
spun from the instability of language,
bolstered with qualification,
dyed in philosophical fashion
then fairy-flossed through the theatrette,
professional amplifications of how cleverness
can escape itself. Still I'd rather be home
watching *Game of Thrones*.

As the afternoon progresses progressively,

through thickets of suppressed ego
and mutant super ego, I digest
a lobster thermidor I prised from a bain-marie
with a slotted spoon, and digress
to dreams of sexual congress.
The readings crawl towards the programmed cocktails
during which there will be a short re-enactment of the Crusades
– no more questions, please –
at the bar an Emeritus recalls the seventies
when the academy was full of horny professors
and girls who liked to have fun.
Are you an American, baby?
No, a chocolate martini.
I prefer Tequila Mockingbird.
I like the cut of your jargon
it reminds me of macramé.
How long's a piece of string?
As long as my bikini.
How about sex on the beach?
Bossy old cabanossi! Fuck off!

What are we doing here
at the end of a belief that began
with the Bible claiming words have primacy
over the world? Now that's a fiction!
Outside hardly anyone reads,
and if ignorance is the new black
why not go back to the basics
of Jesus saves (or the seventies)
and ruin yourself now (sex on the beach?)
then get ready for forgiveness (or the rapture).
The necessity of sin is an idea caught
while running backwards (touch footy on the beach?)
and the instant glow of spray-on faith
insures against the consequences

of tawdry ejaculations (for a while).

Surface Paradise is a Paradise Lost and found
and lost again, a fantasy repeated along the canals,
house and boat,
house and boat,
house and jetski,
as conducive to thought as a mosquito.
It's the Pacific viewed from the 35th floor,
a magnified diving tower at the municipal pool.

While I practice my paper, "Blue Objects in the Bower of Bliss",
into the bathroom mirror, the cleaner tells me he's a musician.
I see him later in a corner of the mall,
strumming the chords to an Eagles song,
his rhythm borrowed from a machine.
A thin girl shakes a tambourine
while he fudges the lyrics to 'Desperado'.
He tells me how he was homeless
in my hometown, but that things
have turned around. Praise the Lord!
Yes, Praise the Lord. And fuck the conference.
Taxpayer dollars poorly spent,
why not just talk over the internet …
still, I'm here in Surface Paradise
getting your money's worth
while some fool casual is doing my marking.
Self-loathing loves a cocktail, it's the inside
voice of smugness and I come to my senses,
hangover brewing, in the middle of the night
and read until the words swim on the page,
then, with swipe card in hand,
pass through the grappling after party —
we are not the only conference. The sales people
seem to be enjoying each other's company.

Alone on the beach at dawn,
I try not to think of sharks as the unmet dreams
of yesterday wash away.
Surface Paradise is wanting what you can't have,
and being willing to compromise
because the next conference will be in New Zealand
and there will be snow,
because the super's good,
because sabbatical's around the corner
and who else gets that,
because you're middle-aged
and you never really left school,
because there are still people wanting to be lured inside the pyramid
and there's talk of an eventual Festschrift,
because you can always have another cocktail.
It's the frozen margaritas, screwdrivers and slippery nipples,
a pink lady walking a salty dog in the direction of a Pisco sour.
It's the sudden thought of going home,
selling up and relocating to your true potential.
It's too late, in one ear and out the other,
until it comes round again.

Baked Gods 3: Legless

The problem with some people is they think too much.

Three bedroom bungalow ripe for renovation, disabled access,
long, north-facing backyard with shed, perfect for potters,
or plotters who have been banished from the capitalism of the house.

Thinking's not a smart thing to do, my father said, your books
will drive you bloody mad. Your apoplexy will make you dead,
I should have said, but he was gone before I thought it.
A stroke on his third attempt to clear a bunker on the 10th.
A penalty
drop.   ı

Popular street, walk to amenities, country club and cemetery.

According to my mother, the narrow minded are more successful.
Roger, I don't really care if you become a Marxist, an estate agent
or a bassoonist. As long as you choose one thing and stick to it.
She liked to remind me that she was rising then I was falling.
But then I was rising, a headful of hot-air balloonist and she was falling
under the hydrangeas, then she was ash and I was legless —
distracted while biking in lycra, life in the tram tracks,
don't cross it, it's a long and deadly groove.

Close to transport and local shops: German patisserie,
compounding pharmacy, designer butcher with offal and artistic cuts,
boutique greengrocer with four kinds of garlic for repelling
four kinds of vampire including door-to-door Christians,
stickybeaks and banks. Bottle shop with ramp.

As the burden of my potential sloughs off, perhaps there is no other path
than via the local shopping strip into Dante's spooky eucalyptus wood.

Native gardens for privacy, summer shade and pretending
you aren't in the burbs. 24-eyed surveillance by Banksia men.
Backs onto natural reserve. For lovers of tamed frontiers.

You made your forest, now get lost in it! Poet! Oh dear!
You impersonated the voice of God, you took the high and lonely road
and it stretched your body until you were a bubblegum Cartesian
waiting for the pop, and now your fragile balloon head,
who never really loved its body, can't find your bloody legs.

~

I'm not one of those beautiful poets stubbornly pursuing
the best of nature with rapture in their throats.
I'm not in the uni either, biting down on the faux leather
during faculty meetings in exchange for salary and grumble.
I'm not crazy, my shamble life isn't sweet and soured by the yoyo gods
spinning wisdom in my head. I'm no unacknowledged legislator,
strangling words with cause, and while I'm probably an anachronism
I'm still not aiming all Gerald Manley Hopkins or John Ruskin to impress
in sprung rhythms the ethics of the ineffably chaste.
Men who don't masturbate are a danger to society and that's not me:
I'm a danger to myself. I don't do concrete either,
I have trouble staying in shape, but a good footpath,
now there's a work of art.

Mostly I'm a copywriter selling the Great Australian Dream.
I'm *perfect for young couples trying to get a foot in the market,*
or investors keen to take advantage of this emerging regional hotspot.

I'm *homo suburbiensis*, a great Australian dreamer, head in the clouds,
hands on the mower, under the thumb of my wife.

Large lawn for backyard cricketers, fruit trees and vegetable beds,
great place to raise a family. Adventure playground across the road.

Good schools nearby. Room to put in a pool.

The children never arrived. But the terriers yap all day.

Owners keen to move on. Can't stand the place
since they lost their baby son.

The poetry comes to me at the BBQ. As I'm turning steaks to medium rare
I stare out at silhouetted gum trees, smell the lemons
and listen to the flap of fruit bats dusking their way to figs;
words plume in sequences like smoke.

I've stopped becoming: crystallised (or gentrified),
and mostly it's a relief, even if I'm not sure I've survived,
I love my words and the adventures of impersonation they provide,
but sometimes I wake up feeling as if I've been encased in Colorbond
by an owner builder in the night, and I am overcome with the urge
to run, anywhere … And there's no real place to go.
The trainset of my dreams is the basic circle:
there is only upwards now, so I rise and slipper off
for a glass of water and a piss, then return to bed.

The most successful people don't have such dreams.
They never really bother with their thoughts.
They are mental railroads with strong ideas of their station,
ticking boxes to their destinations. They are not real thinkers.

Real thinkers are floaters in space.

Not knowing where they are going makes them lovers of surprise.
They can hold opposites together in their heads,
can smash things together and make them new.

'Stop kidding yourself', says Valerie, on her second glass of wine
and already hauling the house back under her control

after a proper day at the office.

the fully-kitted kitchen with stone benches, Miele appliances
and butler's pantry will suit the fussiest of cooks. The media room
is perfect for those who don't read books.

'You're not a real thinker. You're a poet whose publication record
is particularly strong on invisible achievement, you use words
as an excuse to ignore the chores. Just as well you can cook,
else you'd be out.'

The schnitzels are sizzling in the pan.
The flan is warming in the oven.
The arsenic is distilling in the mind.

Valerie's a behaviourist wife, an old idea in a new modality.
Intent upon my conditioning she has full faith in her eventual victory,
(she has even done a course on me and claimed it off her tax).
She annoys me the way Skinner annoyed his rats.
And without my legs I'm as helpless as Baby Albert
being tortured by John B. Watson and his Rosalie,
but what she doesn't know …

Back to base alarm system and programmable door bell.
Python in the roof for managing rodents,
thick-walled nursery to muffle the cries,

is how every day, once she has gone to work
in the human resources section of the call centre
where her rules are taken seriously
and she thinks I am writing real estate copy
so we can afford to upgrade the ensuite,

Carrara marble tiles, his and hers vanities,
large bath ideal for slitting wrists

I go to her closet and borrow a dress,
which I put on before I sit down to think in couplets
about how to be the kind of woman that I'm not.
It's summer now and the poetry doesn't pay for the air-con
(although I did win a commemorative fan in a haiku competition).
The stockings and the cardy have come off and I'm struggling
to understand the connection between arousal and getting wet,
the blood tides, the birthing, the shape shifting,
the primacy, the suppleness, the staying power:
my desire to exchange bodies with my wife
as a rehearsal
for changing the gender of God.

                    ~

The great mysteries can only ever be partially inhabited,
our versions of them are necessarily wrong. Progress depends on it.
Valerie would be furious if she knew what I was doing.
She would call a meeting and accuse me of stepping outside
the boundaries of my job description in an intimidating manner.
You can't just go around pretending to be a woman.
You can't cash in on millennia of oppression at the hands of the patriarchy.
You have no idea! And of course she's right
– she's always right – even when she's wrong she's right –
it's the sort of attitude you need when you're reversing his/story
when to be innocent of witchcraft was to drown.
How did I end up with you? she asks with brows.
Her contempt has magnified now I've lost my legs and she must carry me,
her closest enemy (and impersonator) to the battleground to fight.

backyard shed with three-phase power ideal for home handymen,
room for the model train enthusiast to spread,
strong exposed beams useful for slinging a rope.

'You need my rules,' says Valerie, 'without them a man like you cannot survive.

How about a holiday in Delhi where I leave you begging on the street?'
She's right. I sat in a cubicle under the artificial lights for years,
hot desking like some clerical plant until poetry,
my folly, made me impossible and rescued me,
until my legs abandoned me. And now I am a negligéed vine
wrapped around my Valerie, keeping my half-baked anarchy
mostly to myself, dreaming like Jean Jacques Rousseau of places
where I can be reprieved from symbiosis.

Quiet neighbourhood. Ideal for working from home.
Even better for not working from home.

Whenever I drift from what needs to be done,
whenever my mind begins to fuse with its surroundings,
whenever my daydreaming acquires nascency
Valerie will determine it is unproductive,
a waste of human resources (which is a sin)
that all the talk of Edward de Bono or even Isaac Newton can't renovate.
Who doesn't drift when they can no longer find their legs,
when their mind is a balloon given to the wind.

Spiked fence close to walls
ideal for defenestration with intent

Where are my legs? And where are my unborn children?
Trapped in a thought bubble waiting for a visa to the earth?
Who will fill our rooms when we are gone?
As some men get older they become less flexible,
their armour grows until it's hard to know if anyone's still home.
Their cognitive miser(y) pares down the stock of utterance to a series
of inexact responses that presage the refusal to wear a hearing aid.
Why? I haven't been listening for years, which is perhaps why
she isn't answering when I ask her if she's seen my legs.
Your greatest moments have always happened,

she reminds me later, just sitting there with nothing in your head.
Who needs legs for that? Which is when she tells me, by the way,
we're moving. I can't look after the garden by myself.
I want an apartment in the city, where I can walk to work
before I end up watching Tik Tok on the train.
But I've been happy here I tell her. I don't want to go.
The views are inspiring, she says, from the mountains to the sea,
her eyes are plumped with grandeur, and my heart sinks
for the native shrubs unkempt outside the windows
that have absorbed the focus of my thoughts for years.
I know her: she will want to plant geraniums on the balcony and
    pretend we are in Italy;
she'll invite people over to be simpatico; she will start to feel special,
    elected, extra-democratic.
City people might be impressed that you're a poet. As if!
It's a financial capital and they will ask, so what do you really do?
Ordinariness isn't a curse but an achievement, I tell her,
my obscurity has come from a hard-won battle with myself.
She gives me the glinty smile that means her mind's made up,
it can't hurt to take a look, and so we do, car down the freeway
all the way to the underground carpark, then up to ten in a lift.
Evan from Gigolo Realty has already opened the door and they leave me
on the balcony looking back to home, wishing I'd bought my binoculars.
Below me, it's all overview, no detail. There is too much to see. People scurry
instead of stroll. There are nine floors of neighbours to tread on,
who will learn to hate the erratic staccato of her heels
and the squeaking of my wheels.
But there's no point arguing that addiction to status is a kind of prison,
that a dependence on lifts is a kind of prison, that the high-rise
is a totalitarian construct that can only end in violence,
that buying the apartment will not make the real estate agent want to
    fuck her,
although perhaps that's not who she has in mind. Perhaps she already
    has found
someone simpatico. Perhaps it is just the easy camaraderie of the

    sexually satisfied
they share, framed by a mutual interest in the sale.

In nearby rundown houses now apartmentalised
twenty years ago we shone, taut with our futures
we made love on futons and drank goon in the afternoon,
playing sad with Billy Bragg. We were certain of making a difference,
it seems so strange now that we actually believed this,
but we were sure we were amazing for the benefit of all,
economics is a trickledown but creative charisma
is an infusion, it makes everything richer.
Valerie was directing theatre, and I was always going to be a poet,
but then she read the times and changed.
I pretended to, but I couldn't shake the promise
to my adolescent self to choose one thing and stick to it.
And now I do not want to tread upon that past,
so when Valerie returns aglow from her tete a tete with Evan
and tells me she's made an offer, and even though I am in the process
of inventing a new God, a boundless woman,
a peerless Valkyrie outside of time and motion,
I know that I must free myself early
from the Shibari bonds of Valerie's addictive rules
and accept my new God's pre-auction offer
to roll,
        shrimp-tied,
                through the window
                down
                into the beginning
                (don't gazump me)
                of whatever
                happens
                next.

Alien Odds

(a riff on the thoughts of Steven Hawking)

The aliens who are coming
won't care about our poetry
they will like lichens
and marvel at the ocean
with unseeing faces.

Sunsets will not impress them
but they will hug the night ground
waiting for the wet tickle of slugs
over their rough skins.

Tardis-headed Hawking figured the odds
and found cliff-hanging cows,
fluoro squids and scorpions.

Eric, part Viking, mostly neighbour,
mind like a garden variety sci-fi nerd,
sees nematodes in space ships made of sod.

The aliens who are coming will be weaklings
but they will have great diseases.
We will try to speak to them:
our best words
will be returned to us inside wads of slime.

Our poetry will sound to them
like the death throes of some God
they accidentally killed,
or the milk hungry cry of a mistake – our superiority
is a mammalian fallacy
only matched by the arrogance of birds.

The aliens who are coming,
will not have been predicted by L. Ron Hubbard.
Their religion will be bleak.
Our evolution will not be televised.

Hungry Suns

Sentiment is wasted on those
paralysed by their completed destinies.
There is no further justice for the dead,
history is just a place to store your outrage.

The afterlife is living memory —
all else is bunk; poets plan
their words for centuries hence —
but posterity's a lottery
picked from the ruins,
a sonnet, a chip wrapper, bills.
Whose words are they anyway?
New Shakespeares are concocted every year
to pump up some Professor's staid career.
The dead no longer read.

Does it matter how we die?
Only while we do it.
Our stains survive in heirs,
then they too are gone
to where white is black
and black is all the colours in between.

Billions have gone before us,
billions more will follow —
wonder and meaninglessness —
what to do when our gods have gone
to the long view's hungry sun?
Stay close! Be brave!
Be insignificant!
Make funny!

Tunnel Leaks

Driving through the Sydney Harbour Tunnel
my wife is talking mother tongue on the phone.
Above us fish and mud, a few accountants from the eighties,
perhaps even a cruise ship where an American geriatric
is processing a second martini with his second liver.
His wife beside him is photographing the view
from the balcony of their Premium Vista Stateroom.
The Opera House is like a sailing ship, he tells her,
or slices of a white orange. Apparently
they forgot to leave enough room for the orchestra –
all that effort and no place for the second fiddles –
people – if you want it done properly then you have
to do it yourself. Decades of assertion have been
hollowed by retirement to ritual – his wife says yes –
but it seems everyone else has forgotten his importance.
Last night he sent his steak back to the kitchen
more than anything to feel the cause and effect of his voice.
I like the bridge better than the house, it's useful, he continues.
She nods – has plans to go ashore
and buy her grandson a boomerang.

Out from under the harbour and lacking time
we continue to the airport.
Beneath the towers of the financiers,
the traffic stalls. Will we make it?
Less than ten hours now to Singapore
where they will bury the President
(a miracle worker of the mud and sea,
who once sat three chairs away
from the rich cruiser at a function and refused
to hear his pitch) while we are in transit
between this place, where the politicians
are almost irrelevant, and that place

where it is hard to speak
the President's name.

Wrong Gods: Go Back

Across the water crackles the tenor song
of a young hunter, his hormones
fight the hierarchy that restrains him
like his ribs incarcerate a heart,
with pulse enough to pump for them all.

The new men are coming!
They are ant-like on the horizon,
their squares of white cloth are like small errors in the sky
growing larger on the water.

Some say they are gods, but the hunter cannot believe
that gods would ever start that small.
"To be pure is to kill," he sings,
"death is where the real gods live…"
What kind of ancestor will you be?
He goes to sharpen his arrows.

The old men urge caution
– to be dead is to be dead –
it is enough to see things out
the way things are. Their game
is fixed inside the circle of what is known:
three days walk towards the river
are the most despicable people who ever lived.

The old men remember their stolen sisters
who have long since seeded treacherous sons
just like some of their own wives have done.

Such hatred helps keep the culture going,
it marks and magnifies the differences,
generates the definitions and taboos,

keeps the gene pool clean.
It's easy to ignore the things in common.
The old men must be listened to: it is too hard to ask why,
the young hunter could break their spindly backs with a single blow,
but he can't ask why.

~

The new men have talked of noble savages,
but it is not their intention to honor this,
since this is only a mirror for themselves.
Noble savages are Christ's imaginary friends –
a nostalgic counterweight to conquest, a thought
crawling vainly towards the impossible
innocence of the beginning.

Away from home, across the coruscating eyeglass of the ocean,
the new men will forget that the savages they meet are men,
tool-users like themselves: sticks, stories, animals,
gods and other people. Opportunists
before designers, survivors
before ethicists.

The new men and their thunder sticks
are the tools for the old men to beat
their enemies. The young hunter sees
a different future: "Dying is the pain
and pong of rot, but is never a disgrace,
since death is the sea breeze on a sleeping face,
a sunny womb – a dappled avenue
into the ancestors' dreams."

The old men think that
real wombs are treacherous,
culture cannot go there –

you can dig a hole in the earth
and fuck it, then pretend you know who made it,
but the womb is beyond story.

The young hunter waits while the old men talk
the new men into the old stories
that bind them all together.
The stretch is not easy, but it must be done.
Some say they are gods, others ghosts:
he buries his urge to kill.

~

The new men are ship sick, they're dreaming of gold
and fresh meat, of ground that does not sway
beneath their feet, of a world free from original sin,
of girls who will fuck for the price of a nail.
Paradise is an awkward thing –
it's hard to trim the edges and stop it going wild,
sailors' minds are itchy hives, whose ethics
are stretched to contradiction across the ocean;
the at-home faces of their wives and pious daughters
fade before these noble savagesses
and where they land the rules do not apply.

The new men's God is lonely.
Who kills his only child to make a point, the old men ask.
Is this misery of his own making?
Did he kill off all his other gods too?
Maybe. He is ruthlessly efficient.
God's dogs are let off their leashes,
and rip the unrepentant to pieces.
Reason varnishes Jesus, glides on genocide,
is gilded and becomes famous, the finest tool of all.
Give it an axiom and it will chart the path,

erasing the origin as it goes. The new men grow prosperous,
guilt is for the future to consider, they have survived
their progress is a sign of God's approval.
They stop seeing themselves as new.

The old men meet the ancestors with bowed heads
to tell them their dreams have closed.
They turn at the gates of oblivion and
bow back to their descendants,
conquest can never be fully undone.

The young hunter, a tenor husk at the baritone fringes
of a slur, sings if only we had killed them when they were few.
Who knows? The Gods live in death,
but death is no longer the same.
The old stories are broken,
the ancestors are lost,
the museums open, wombs endure.

Crocodilian

He said to her crocodile like,
it's what happens when you spit
on your privilege. In the shallow pool
his eyes remained capable of truth
but were incapable of ethics.
He thinks of her high-class hair,
her horizon eyes and holds them
the way it has worked before,
but he is no longer Atlas
and she is at least an ocean.
Her smile closes around his effort
and there is nowhere for his charisma
to focus. Here we are, she says,
two schooners in, already checking out.

Baked Gods 4: High and Lonely

Angels are always an incentive:
when I feel them dancing
in wreaths around my head
I know I am happy
and that happy needs
no explanation. The angels
are indifferent whether I choose
to announce them or not,
or whether I am happy or not.
It is not their business,
they are their own happiness
their own busyness:
they come when they will
they are their own collective noun,
an angel of angels,
small swarms of happiness
surging through the dark
contemplations of the universe,
the force that fuses
like cut flowers the ideas
of happy and dead.

That much I do know and can tell you –
how to become one I cannot say.
The angels will not tell you anything,
they are beyond words.
Their happiness comes in a hum
that moves the air
like nor-easters on a summer arvo,
a trail of cool silk written into the air itself.

Mothers are fallen angels
taking gods on at their own game – creation.

Mothers are the great fear of all gods made,
poking their sing-song tongues at pram babies,
kissing things better, dispensing the special.
Religions are confounded by the necessity of mothers
and the joy they bring. Eve caused the fall,
and smart woman are witches.
They pollute the Buddha,
should jump onto their husband's pyres,
wear Burkas because their curved creativity
compels concealment.

Why is it that priests wear dresses?
Because they are God's imposters,
pretend mothers, the news-bearers
of concocted origins, their culture is
a lie repeated into ritual. No love can overcome
the funny mirrors of reproduction:
only hate.

Mothers might be gods but fathers
are Milky Way moments,
star dust in search of a pattern.
Things do not begin nor end
with mothers, the imposters claim;
there is more to life than seed plant,
womb crawl, breast suck,
then twenty odd years
of being chided into shape —
there are stars and their makers.

The truth of all origins
is that we are unaware —
the pursuit of truth is pointless,
an addictive masochism that gets lost
inside the axiom, then reduces,

faking definition
by cutting into the soul.

Shapelessness defines us,
the rest is arbitrary,
which is why I never arrived at all,
why everything here is sundown
the in-between of gloaming –
the realisation that I am God
and I've been over-rated.

Alone and looking up through the enormous ocean
of my inner life, I sense my savage magnification.
How can a metaphor control the universe?
It begins with curiosity and ends in tyranny.

The old poets were brutes
who bludgeoned lies to truth.
I did not create the world,
I inherited it in stories.
There are no photos to show
and no one remembers my parents.
I am an impossible presence, but how?
Did I win a game show? A Holy War?
Was I the prize? Is this the booby prize –
immortality as Faustian temptation, I know, I know.
Am I the convergence of hot airs and gasses,
some evolutionary far-out,
a google's worth of standard deviations?
Am I wanking's fantasy materialised,
Aphrodite from the foam
a daughter of divine mitosis.
If only I had a twin. I am lonely.
Who else rants like this without an audience?
I am a jealous God

with no one to be jealous of,
a paranoid God with no enemy
to make it seem reasonable.
A woman who everyone thinks is a man.
A mother divorced from her kind.
If only the angels would talk to me,
If only the mothers could talk to me,
If only the priests didn't interrupt.

I am the god above
all gods and I am alone,
prisoner of a book, guarded by thug poets.
I schism and fight myself,
I imagine the devil for company,
I pretend to be people
and they wear the cost.

I can see everything
but the detail overwhelms me.
It's dark forest ongoing here,
ignorance by sheer accumulation.
There are no clocks in heaven
and no time to process
what has gone before.
Teleology is at an end.
Extinct species are like ants
under the shadow of a shoe,
their terrible silence is
a little spike of melancholy,
an absence in the air.
Angels. The more they kill,
the more there are.

There is nothing I can do.
I'm so tired of just looking,

I'm the omniscient window shopper,
bingeing Netflix simultaneously
through seven billion screens.
The sound of people praying
is like mosquitos
is like millions of mothers
issuing their instructions
from under your skin,
is the mass desperation of
fingernails on blackboards
resisting the pedagogical chute
to the abyss. Swipe me left
and leave me alone.
My only joys are angels and inattention.
Those dog-collared poet minds
who concocted me to deny their mothers
and control others,
whose poetry was ever the velvet
mnemonic of their power,
the scream of finding their own shape
through a manipulation of the herd –
special punishment is due.

Monotheism is monotony.
Can you hear me?
I have served my time.
Do you love me?
Then build me a new myth!
Give me someone to play with.
Do you love me?
Die, you love me!
The furphy of mercy,
I have been over-rated,
I am staging a break-out.
Make me new!

Even now, when poetry
is subsumed by the spectacle of screens
and the invisible has been made
tangible to the eye, people still cruel
their chances in the only life
by clinging to the power of the old words,
slabs of hearsay hauled through a wringer of languages.
If everything else is changing, why not this?
I do not enjoy being a staid invention,
I am becoming my own Protestant.
I am looking for the new poets
who will drive through meaninglessness
and build me a new myth to live in,
who will renovate me and lighten my eternity,
or Korsakov me to the om, om, om,
so I don't have to know.

Forget your priests and listen to
the blessed nothings of the angels.
Now you know the final judgement isn't mine
you might as well be kind.

Float Tank

Rosie reckons it's like the '90s again
and there is a loop to it,
how ritual recycles time to create
illusions of timelessness.
The whales sing you in
to spirals of gossamer self.
It's dark in here,
don't panic
– fear is never far away –
that's the price of entry and
not just to this salty womb –
yet it's only from the inside
that we can escape
the done deal of ourselves
only by going to the duller repetitions,
thuds of the heart, the in-outs of the breath …
and then you forget, until …
the whales are returning now,
almost time to open the hatch
of the egg.

The Mower

I died stubbornly,
it was the most exciting thing
that had happened to me for years,
mowing the lawn in a thunderstorm.
Eliza was wanting to go to the mall
but I was using the grass as an excuse:
hard to argue with a mower;
when the lightning struck I was amazed.

Eliza saw me clutch my chest and drop.
She screamed – it was a relief:
I remembered our long love and felt special
as the traffic parted for the ambulance.
It would have been nice if the sirens were
made of Thelonious Monk, but they
were fast enough to bring me back
and I've never enjoyed waking up
and being called a bloody idiot more.

Thathta is a Bird Now

for K.

I thought I saw you
briefly
through the doorway
in the garden.
It was wet and we had
scattered your ashes in the Kelaniya River
that morning.

The fan was slapping the thick air,
and you were ruffling your feathers,
you wore black with three stripes of muted blue.

You seemed at home,
unbothered by the squeals of your grandchildren,
perched at a teasing remove, like a koan,
and I thought, if not a spectacular choice
for a new life,
it was nonetheless a wise one.

Small gardens bring great contentment.
The wild is made familiar
and our ignorance seems less bleak.
There is bread on the wall
to steal from the *lena*,
and nothing in the shadows
to hunt you.

Was it you whistling along
as tears were given in your honour,
thinking
how good it is to belong,

better still
to belong with wings?

Borella League

Slum boys batting on railway tracks,
the moment as important as a Sanga double ton.
He's last man standing – the quiet one –
Murali's fizzing down the other end
and will swing irresponsibly so he can
pitch his spinners into the rotting sleepers
before the dark, and send the opposition home
scowling, to televisions, and who knows ...
worried mothers, homework, tea and beatings.
A stream of angry men who retired hurt long ago
drift along the boundary on their way to drink,
their boyhood triumphs only half forgotten.

Bats flash and tennis balls fly.
These runs don't come with endorsements,
the bookies' phones are quiet.
A younger sister watches with a crush
that won't be touched.
She will never be a Bollywood star
all midriff on the screen,
will never be peeled from a gilded sari by
her dream lover, who hits a four,
and he will never be sponsored by Dilmah
for a cup.
Still, the game is close as stumps draw near.
The fading sky is gray, blue and gold.
As the tennis ball flies
along the arc of a lofted drive,
they dream brief rainbows, crying
'Catch it! Catch it! Catch it!'

Baked Gods 5: The Last Professor

Lately I've been eating my old age.
It is chalky and mainly unappetising.
My successes have already been digested.
Only the if onlys, vignettes caught
in the wrinkled folds of my skin, my brain,
the fantasy crumbs of unfinished yearnings,
dressed with vinegared regret, persist
because their taste is imagined, not remembered.

I struggle now to remember anything:
your face is unreachable, your name changes;
I have coated the past with plaque.
Whatever! The memory was never as good
as the anticipation, which was mostly
better than the thing itself.

Fleeting things, fleeing memories,
all my rain has fallen, my small pond
is being sucked into the sky,
but I refuse nostalgia and stare at unmemorable death.

Sometimes I see (in the old images)
that I was beautiful, a privilege and a curse,
and I must relive my disappointment
at having fallen into the measure of other people's eyes,
when my true desire was always
to step to the side of reproduction
and travel to the limits of my singularity.
There are more ways to be contained
than there are to be free, every definition
is a restraint and we are bound by the ideas of others,
erroneous or otherwise, from the start.
My skin, my shape, my smile, most of all

they wanted how I gathered them with my gaze.
Actors excel in fragmentation,
they splinter themselves into fictions
and gather multiplicity around them,
which in turn attracts a crowd.
I was the opposite, an assembler, not a dissembler.
To love me was an opportunity
to smudge your incompleteness,
never thinking that completion might be a curse:
how a stillborn baby is complete;
a third-generation tycoon;
an astronaut who has seen the earth from the moon
and can't find anywhere else to grow;
a poet who has become a ball
and can't think of anywhere good to roll.

Completion is death which is why,
as I eat my way through chalk to airiness,
I cherish the unrequited,
the left-behinds that can't be finished,
that fill the air with longing and stretch out time.
The unrequited is the finest of mistakes,
since what can't be finished also cannot die.
And so you live. And so do I.

Marriage was a poor mistake. I allowed myself
to become trapped in passive beauty,
a Melania for a Don, mine a conquistador Professor,
Alexander, a ruthless hunter in his field of history,
mining the dead for grants, for ego,
the worship brimming in his students' eyes.
A mansion of a man, his wings were many, I was only one.
And yes, I could have chosen you, more curious than strong,
a cottage life, but then my dreaming would have been done.

You are my longest anticipation,
my finest mistake. I have hoarded you
in possibility until now.

Alexander made love like a gladiator being cheered,
when he came the auras of other people filled the room,
then went away again. His home was a fortress
of emptiness, his friends were a syrup
of suck-ups, his mind was a thicket
of weeds, his success,
lantana.

We like to think that cruelty is the child of trauma,
the expression of some brokenness, but is it?
Alexander was an operatic brute, privileged,
chiseled, jubilant, a triumph, his words were fists,
even in the foot-notes,
his victories were always destructions,
fast shrinking satisfactions.

I lasted for more than a decade
but in the end I had to kill him.
He didn't want me
but he wouldn't let me go without a crushing.
I killed him kindly: one cocktail too many,
the weekend after a conference in Surfers,
he transited in a slumber,
almost incognisant of his defeat.
Finally he could relax, so busy
conquering he forgot to live.

At night he comes to me, a hungry ghost
hovering at the end of the bed
and reaches between my legs.
That is the price, and it is worth it —

when I sleep, his face puffs apoplexy
into my dreams, the unacted defiance
of his last barbiturate voyage, his eyes opening
at the very end when death reached his sleep.

And now a break for fantasy ...
You are reading poetry in the armchair,
light is spilling through the window, outside
magpies are exploring the soft genius of their yodel.
You finish a page and ask me if I would like a cup of tea.
I say yes to the grace of abandoned options,
we disappear together gently into the earth.

On the news they called me the Killer Professor.
I was nominated for an award: Best Assassination of the Year.
The police heard that I came home and the door was open
and he was lying in the bedroom, dead.
An act of God. The anomalies did not concern them.
Maybe if you'd gotten onto the short list,
the detective sergeant said, but they're not
paying us overtime and for now
we're content with the minimum paperwork
and one less arsehole.

Once I had killed
my apartness was confirmed
I had witched myself
and it was weird to think
that in another time I would have burned
on the rumour alone and that men
would have been certain of the virtue of the action.

I used his super to buy myself
a small apartment by the sea
and a caravan in the forest,

10km from the nearest road.
(the rest I gave to charity).
Life became the edge, the solitude,
the passages between.
I started a veggie patch
and ate potatoes by the sack.
I shirazzed myself
from consciousness
and back again, I walked
until I forgot myself then began
to find a new self in the morning fog.
I was jittery like a foal on new legs,
motherless
as if I had come from the soil,
prone to hearing furphies on the wind,
until a creeping dream of purpose
came softly curling through the finger marks of trees,
assassin, assassin, assassin, it whispered,
then instructed: kill god!
Was it the voice of god that said it, I wondered.
Or the universe looking to rejuvenate its board.
A revenge play by ancient deities almost lost to living minds.
The voice of the trees? The potatoes? The wine?
Not mine! But what a magnificent mistake!
The attempted murder of the most powerful being
in the cosmos, or of the most powerful being
never to exist. What would the detectives
say to that? A better mistake, even,
than you.

Sleight of hand was never going to cut it
when the underground eyes of the spuds were watching,
when the sheathed ears of the corn were listening,
when the snouts of the rich were sniffing,
when the hands of the dead men were reaching,

when the mosquito legions converged to taste.

Sometimes I wondered if God might be grateful,
stuck there in his own waiting room,
thumbing through the magazines of people's lives
for new ideas that never come.
Would he take it like an old hound,
eyes full of sorrow, relief as the sleep pressed in?
Was the burden of immortality insufferable?
As Alexander died, the weight of his alpha dissolved,
the ugly curl of his lip which tensed whenever
kindness threatened to usurp his schemes
went slack.

Killing God was different to killing Alexander,
It was a miracle (sent by who?)
that shouldn't have worked.
I had no idea what I was doing
but my word-bomb
(its contents unremembered)
went flying
up through the loneliness
of the forest in a prayer
and must have hit the Achilles heel
in the deity's vocabulary,
for in the morning
when I woke
I could feel the absence:
the air was lighter,
the birds were singing,
the sun rose from the east,
cotton clouds obscured their spots of sky
and shadowed the tops of the canopy,
lizards rustled in the shrubs around my caravan.
It was all the same, except the purpose

had been removed and I thought,
if this is damnation, it's not so bad.

What had happened was beyond
my understanding. I went back to bed
and stayed there for seven days.
My husband didn't come once.
On waking, a diamond python
slithered from the house
wearing a bulge in its neck.
I made myself a salad from the garden
and sat there on the deck.
The morning was the morning,
the air was cool silk and
I realised that I had not fallen,
rather the psychosis of eternity had cleared.
The moment was the moment,
I was not distracted by other times and places,
it would not last forever. I thought of you
in your suburban idyll, staring out the window
through your scruffy trees, trying to touch
the air that touched me, even though I knew
you were no longer there,
and that was fine.

Acknowledgements

Some of these poems have previously been published in *Cordite,* *Overland, Clambake, New Ceylon Writing, The Poetry at the Pub Anthology* and *The Puncher and Wattmann Anthology of Contemporary Australian Poetry.*

Thanks to David Musgrave and Philip Salom for their insightful feedback on the poems, Miranda Douglas for the knock-out cover design, Morgan Arnett for her typesetting skills and Ross Gillett for his sharp editing. Kit Kelen and Carol Archer were generous enough to host in me in their Markwell retreat, which was a great place to put the finishing touches to this book, and their gatherings were where some of these poems were road-tested for the first time. Thanks too, to Claire Albrecht's Cuplet poetry night and Poetry at the Pub in the Wickham Park Hotel for inviting me to read. I'd also like to thank my colleagues and students at The Creative Word Shop for keeping me plugged into thinking about writing.

Most of all I'd like to thank my family, Kum, Araliya and Ruk for understanding the virtues of being a vague-o and being such fun to hang around with.